Dr. Ant[...] [...] on Hot Seat: The Latest Controversies Explained

Everything You Need to Know About Why He is Making Headlines

By

Brittany Jones

Table of Content

Introduction

Dr. Anthony Fauci, the former Director of the National Institute of Allergy and Infectious Diseases and a leading figure during the COVID-19 pandemic, has once again become the center of media attention. This time, his recent testimony before the House Select Subcommittee on the Coronavirus Pandemic has sparked a flurry of debates and controversies.

This book centers on what happened, the issues at hand, and why Dr. Fauci is making headlines. We'll break down the key points of his testimony, the allegations against him, and the different perspectives from both sides of the political spectrum.

If you're a Democrat, Republican, or simply someone interested in understanding the current discussions around Dr. Fauci, this book aims to provide a clear and straightforward explanation of the situation.

1

Dr. Anthony Fauci (Background)

Dr. Anthony Fauci is a well-known infectious disease expert who has served the public for over 50 years. He has advised multiple presidents on health issues like AIDS, Ebola, and the flu. During the COVID-19 pandemic, he became a familiar face, giving daily updates and guidance on how to stay safe.

Born on December 24th 1940, and serving as the director of the National Institute of Allergy and Infectious Diseases (NIAID) from 1984 to 2022, earning him recognition as one of the world's most cited scientists.

Throughout his tenure, Fauci navigated different health crises, including the 2009 swine flu pandemic and the Ebola outbreak in 2014. However, it was during the COVID-19 pandemic that his visibility became popular. As a member of the White House Coronavirus Task Force under President Donald Trump, he became a prominent spokesperson for public health measures, advocating for social distancing and mitigation strategies.

In December 2022, Dr. Fauci retired from his position, but he continues to be a significant figure in discussions about the pandemic and its management.

2

The Hearing: What Really Happened?

During the recent hearing before the House Select Subcommittee on the Coronavirus Pandemic, Dr. Fauci faced rigorous questioning from House Republicans regarding his management of the COVID-19 pandemic. This marked his first public testimony since retiring from government service in December 2022. The hearing was characterized by a barrage of inquiries covering a spectrum of pandemic-related issues, ranging from the contentious origins of the virus to the implementation of mask mandates and vaccination protocols.

Examination of the COVID-19 Origins

One of the pivotal topics addressed during the hearing was the origin of the COVID-19 virus. Dr. Fauci provided insights into the evolving understanding of how the virus emerged, including the possibility of a lab leak from the Wuhan Institute of Virology.

His response: He emphasized the importance of conducting thorough investigations and collaborating with international partners to ascertain the origins of the virus comprehensively.

Mask Mandates and Social Distancing Guidelines

The discussion also veered towards the efficacy and necessity of mask mandates and social distancing guidelines implemented throughout the pandemic.

His response: Dr. Fauci elucidated the scientific rationale behind evolving recommendations, emphasizing the imperative of adapting strategies based on emerging evidence and epidemiological trends. He underscored the importance of balancing public health measures with socio-economic considerations while addressing the committee's inquiries.

Vaccine Policies

Vaccine policies emerged as another focal point of the hearing, with Dr. Fauci addressing inquiries regarding the development, distribution, and administration of COVID-19 vaccines.

His response: He provided insights into the rigorous scientific evaluation and regulatory oversight of vaccine candidates, highlighting the unprecedented speed and collaboration in vaccine development efforts. Dr. Fauci emphasized the critical role of vaccines in curbing the spread of the virus and mitigating the impact of the pandemic globally.

Accusations of Covering Up Information

Accusations of concealing crucial information and misrepresenting facts regarding the pandemic response surfaced during the hearing, prompting Dr. Fauci to provide transparent accounts of his actions and decisions throughout the crisis.

His response: He refuted allegations of withholding data or downplaying the severity of the pandemic, emphasizing his commitment to transparency and evidence-based decision-making. Dr. Fauci reiterated his dedication to fostering public trust and scientific integrity in navigating the complexities of the ongoing pandemic.

Does Dr. Fauci's responses during the recent hearing reflect transparency, scientific rigor, and evidence-based decision-making in addressing the multifaceted challenges posed by the COVID-19 pandemic? Do his testimony provide valuable insights into the complexities of pandemic management while striving to uphold public health

principles and foster public trust in the
ongoing efforts to combat COVID-19

3

Fauci Under Fire: Allegations and Defenses

Republicans accused Fauci of influencing scientists to dismiss the lab-leak theory and using personal email accounts to evade public scrutiny. In response, Fauci vehemently denied these allegations, calling them **"*simply preposterous*"** and asserting his commitment to transparency. He emphasized that he had always encouraged the scientific community to explore all possible origins of the virus.

1. **Influencing Scientists**: Despite allegations from some Republicans suggesting that Dr. Fauci attempted to sway scientists away from concluding that the virus originated from a lab, he adamantly refuted these claims, dismissing them as "***preposterous***."

2. **Cover-Up of Virus Origins**: Accusations arose regarding Dr. Fauci's alleged attempts to conceal the possibility of the virus originating from a lab. However, he countered these claims by presenting emails demonstrating his encouragement for scientists to openly report their findings.

3. **Use of Personal Email for Official Business**: Another point of contention was whether Dr. Fauci used his personal email to avoid public records laws. He denied conducting official business via his personal email.

4. **Gain-of-Function Research**: Questions arose from committee members regarding the funding of research aimed at enhancing virus transmissibility, commonly referred to as *gain-of-function research*. Dr. Fauci clarified that the research supported by funding did not fall under the category of gain-of-function research. This

clarification came amidst ongoing discussions about the origins of COVID-19 and the contentious debate surrounding gain-of-function research. Despite Dr. Fauci's assertions that the viruses studied under NIH funding could not have been responsible for causing the pandemic, Republicans persisted in pressing these issues, advocating for increased scrutiny and oversight.

4

The Political Backdrop

The hearing took place against the backdrop of a contentious election cycle, with Republicans using Fauci as a focal point for their critiques of the pandemic response. Democrats, on the other hand, defended Fauci, accusing Republicans of scapegoating him to divert attention from the early mishandlings of the pandemic.

Republican View

From the Republican perspective, the hearing served as a platform to voice long-standing grievances regarding Dr. Fauci's leadership and management of the COVID-19 crisis. Many Republicans expressed deep skepticism and criticism of Dr. Fauci's approach, citing concerns over what they perceived as a lack of transparency, overreach in decision-making, and a failure to adequately consider alternative viewpoints. Criticisms ranged from accusations of inconsistency in messaging regarding mask mandates and social distancing guidelines to allegations of suppressing dissenting scientific opinions, particularly regarding the lab-leak hypothesis.

One of the primary points of contention raised by Republicans was Dr. Fauci's alleged influence on scientists to dismiss the lab-leak theory as a possible origin of the virus. They argued that his insistence on the natural origins of the virus and dismissal of the lab-leak hypothesis undermined the pursuit of truth and hindered efforts to hold the Chinese government accountable for its role in the pandemic's outbreak. Additionally, they also raised concerns about Dr.

Fauci's use of personal email accounts for official business, alleging that this practice was intended to evade public scrutiny and circumvent transparency laws.

Furthermore, Republicans criticized him for what they perceived as an overly cautious approach to reopening the economy and lifting pandemic restrictions. They argued that his recommendations were overly burdensome and lacked consideration for the economic repercussions, leading to prolonged closures and economic hardship for many Americans. Some Republicans also accused Dr. Fauci of overstepping his authority and encroaching on states' rights by advocating for nationwide mandates rather than allowing for localized decision-making based on individual state circumstances.

Democratic View

In contrast, Democrats rallied behind Dr. Fauci, portraying the hearing as a politically motivated attack orchestrated by Republicans to undermine public confidence in science and deflect blame for the pandemic's challenges. They argued that the focus on Dr. Fauci was a distraction tactic aimed at diverting attention from the failures of the previous administration in handling the pandemic and downplaying its severity.

Democrats emphasized his extensive experience and expertise in infectious diseases, praising his dedication to public service and tireless efforts to combat the pandemic. They highlighted his role as a trusted advisor to multiple administrations, spanning decades of public health crises, and credited him with providing invaluable guidance and leadership during unprecedented challenges.

Furthermore, they also defended him against accusations of influencing scientists to dismiss the lab-leak theory, citing his consistent advocacy for thorough investigations into the virus's origins and commitment to following the science. They argued that attempts to politicize the issue only served to undermine scientific integrity and hinder efforts to understand the true origins of the virus.

Democrats pushed back against allegations of Dr. Fauci using personal email accounts for official business, arguing that such practices were common among government officials and did not constitute wrongdoing. They maintained that Dr. Fauci remained transparent and accountable in his communications, ensuring that relevant information was appropriately documented and accessible to the public.

In all, the hearing shows the deep partisan divisions surrounding Dr. Fauci's role and actions in responding to the COVID-19 pandemic. While Republicans sought to cast doubt on his credibility and hold him accountable for perceived missteps, Democrats mounted up to his defense, portraying him as a dedicated public servant facing unjustified attacks from political adversaries.

5

Personal Toll: Death Threats on Dr. Fauci and His Family

During his testimony, Dr. Fauci became emotional when discussing the death threats he and his family have received. In his exact words, he recounted the harrowing experience:

"Emails, letters, texts to myself, my wife, my three daughters— they have been credible death threats leading to the arrest of two individuals. Credible death

threats mean someone who was clearly on their way to kill me, and it has required my having protective services essentially all the time. It is very troublesome to me, and it is much more troublesome because they involve my wife and three daughters."

When asked by a Congress member how he felt at that moment, Dr. Fauci responded simply, *"Terrible."* The gravity of the situation was palpable, highlighting the personal toll his public role has exacted on him and his family.

In response to further inquiry about ongoing threats, Dr. Fauci affirmed, *"Yes,*

I do. Every time someone gets up and says I'm responsible for the death of people throughout the world, the death threats go up."

While it's true that millions have lost their lives, along with loved ones, do these death threats have the power to effect change? Or are they simply a disturbing consequence of being a public figure targeted in a politically charged debate?

6

The Public's Reaction

The hearing has reignited public debate about the handling of the COVID-19 pandemic.

1. **Supporters of Fauci**: Many supporters of Dr. Fauci see the accusations leveled against him as politically motivated attacks aimed at discrediting his expertise and deflecting blame from other government officials. They argue that Fauci has dedicated his career to public health and has been a leading voice in guiding the country

through the pandemic with scientific evidence and expertise.

2. **Critics**: On the other hand, critics of Fauci and his handling of the pandemic believe that there are still unanswered questions about the early decisions made by health officials, including Fauci himself. They argue that Fauci's guidance has been inconsistent at times and that he may have downplayed certain aspects of the virus's severity or origins.

3. **General Public**: The general public's reaction to the hearing and the controversies surrounding Fauci varies widely. Some people remain steadfast in

their support of Fauci, citing his decades of experience and dedication to public health. Others are more skeptical, expressing concerns about transparency and accountability in the government's pandemic response efforts.

Here's what some individuals on X (Twitter) have to say:

 **Collin Rugg** ✔
@CollinRugg

 Subscribe ⋮

REPORT: Dr. Fauci, who is accused of lying under oath, admits he made up cov*d rules including social distancing & masks for children despite not having scientific data to back it up.

I'm still waiting for the 'no one is above the law' crowd to go after Fauci.

Fauci admits in transcripts released by Republican lawmakers that he was just making rules up as he went.

Question: Do you recall when discussions regarding, kind of, the at least a 6-foot threshold began?

Fauci: You know, I don't recall. It sort of just appeared.

Question: Did you see any studies that supported 6 feet?

Fauci: I was not aware of studies...

Fauci also admitted that he didn't have any research to support masking children but told the American public to mask children anyway.

Question: Did you see any studies that supported 6 feet?

Fauci: I was not aware of studies...

Fauci also admitted that he didn't have any research to support masking children but told the American public to mask children anyway.

Turns out "trust the science" meant trusting someone who was just making stuff up. Shocker.

21   Q   Do you recall when discussions regarding, kind of, the at-least-a-6-foot

22   threshold began?

23   A   The 6-foot in the school?

24   Q   Six-foot overall.   I mean, 6-foot was applied at businesses --

25   A   Yeah.

1   Q   -- it was applied in schools, it was applied here.   At least how the messaging

2   was applied was that 6-foot distancing was the distance that needed to be --

3   A   You know, I don't recall.   It sort of just appeared.   I don't recall, like, a

4   discussion of whether it should be 5 or 6 or whatever.   It was just that 6-foot is --

5   Q   Did you see any studies that supported 6 feet?

6   A   I was not aware of studies that -- in fact, that would be a very difficult study

7   to do.

SOCIAL DISTANCING

3   Q   Do you recall reviewing any studies or data supporting masking for children?

4   A   You know, I might have, Mitch, but I don't recall specifically that I did.   I

5   might have.

6   Q   Since the -- there's been a lot of studies that have come out since the

7   pandemic started, but specifically on this there have been significant on kind of like the

8   learning loss and speech and development issues that have been associated with

9   particularly young children wearing masks while they're growing up.   They can't see

10   their teacher talk and can't learn how to form words.

11   Have you followed any of those studies?

12   A   No.   But I believe that there are a lot of conflicting studies too, that there

13   are those that say, yes, there is an impact, and there are those that say there's not.   I

14   still think that's up in the air.

MASKING

Kim Dotcom ✓
@KimDotcom

Follow

The fall of Fauci. Covid-19 is officially exposed as a US Govt project. A virus engineered by US scientists using a bio lab in China for cover. The biggest crime against humanity killed more victims than the Nazi holocaust against the Jews. Demand Justice.

CAPITOL HILL
LIVE 12:15 PM ET

BREAKING NEWS
NOW: FAUCI TESTIFIES BEFORE HOUSE COVID SUBCMTE
FOX NEWS ALERT

HUNTER BIDEN GUN TRIAL
JURY SELECTION NOW

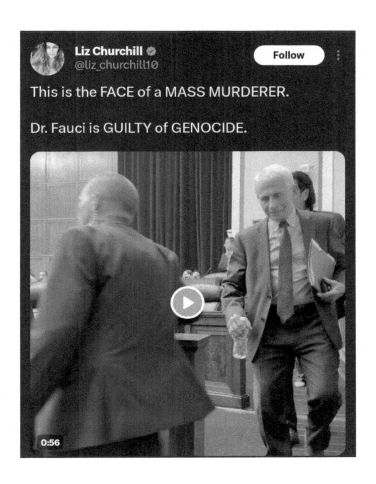

Dr. Simon Goddek ✓ ⬤
@goddeketal

Rep. Jim Jordan: "Wow, Fauci, the smartest man on the planet couldn't remember things 212 times?"

Today, he'll once again claim he remembers nothing to try to cover up that global crime.

Why not apply George W Bush's "enhanced interrogation techniques" to fix his memory lapses?

Liz Churchill ✓
@liz_churchill10

Follow

Dr. Fauci made over $500M from the 'Covid Pandemic' while his Bitch Daughter, Allison, worked at Twitter to censor anyone that opposed her Murderous Father.

≡ Daily**Mail** Politics
.com

REVEALED: Dr. Anthony Fauci confesses he 'made up' covid rules including 6 feet social distancing and masking kids

f   ○   ●   ↥

💬 **351** comments

📷 +8
View gallery

End Wokeness ✓
@EndWokeness

Under oath, Fauci admits that he forced our kids to wear masks for no reason.

For this alone, he belongs behind bars.

For life.

3	Q	Do you recall reviewing any studies or data supporting masking for children?
4	A	You know, I might have, Mitch, but I don't recall specifically that I did. I
5	might have.	
6	Q	Since the -- there's been a lot of studies that have come out since the
7	pandemic started, but specifically on this there have been significant on kind of like the	
8	learning loss and speech and development issues that have been associated with	
9	particularly young children wearing masks while they're growing up. They can't see	
10	their teacher talk and can't learn how to form words.	
11	Have you followed any of those studies?	
12	A	No. But I believe that there are a lot of conflicting studies too, that there
13	are those that say, yes, there is an impact, and there are those that say there's not. I	
14	still think that's up in the air.	

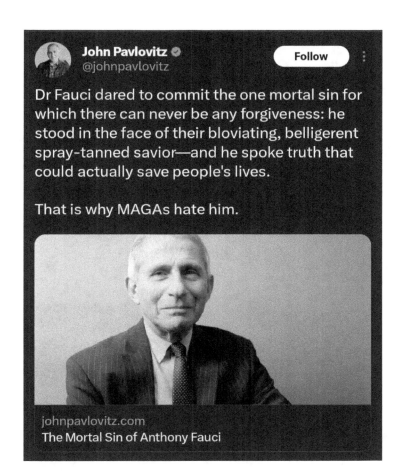

John Pavlovitz ✔
@johnpavlovitz

Follow

Dr Fauci dared to commit the one mortal sin for which there can never be any forgiveness: he stood in the face of their bloviating, belligerent spray-tanned savior—and he spoke truth that could actually save people's lives.

That is why MAGAs hate him.

johnpavlovitz.com
The Mortal Sin of Anthony Fauci

Luke Beasley ✓
@lukepbeasley

Follow

Who else agrees Dr. Fauci is an American hero?

6:24 pm · 03 Jun 24 · **322K** Views

2,745 Reposts **257** Quotes **30.3K** Likes

44 Bookmarks

I Meme Therefore I Am 🇺🇸 ✓ @ImMeme0 · 5h
Replying to @lukepbeasley
A dog torturer and killer can only be a hero to over-vaccinated Democrats.

4   ⟲16   ♡230   ᵢₗᵢ 3.1K   🔖 ⤴

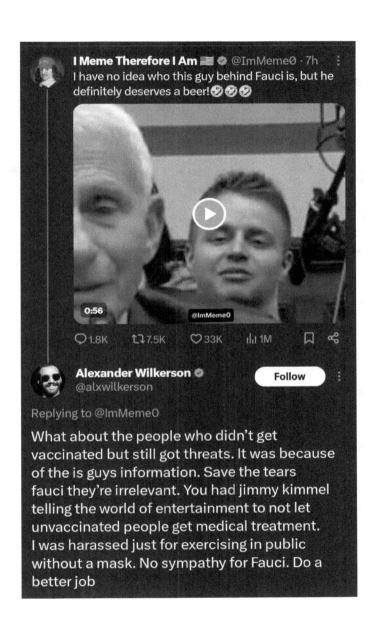

I Meme Therefore I Am 🏴 ✓ @ImMeme0 · 7h

I have no idea who this guy behind Fauci is, but he definitely deserves a beer! 🍻 🍻 🍻

0:56

@ImMeme0

💬 1.8K   🔁 7.5K   ♡ 33K   📊 1M   🔖   ⌁

Alexander Wilkerson ✓
@alxwilkerson

[Follow]

Replying to @ImMeme0

What about the people who didn't get vaccinated but still got threats. It was because of the is guys information. Save the tears fauci they're irrelevant. You had jimmy kimmel telling the world of entertainment to not let unvaccinated people get medical treatment. I was harassed just for exercising in public without a mask. No sympathy for Fauci. Do a better job

Andrew G. Huff, PhD, MS 🇺🇸 ✓   Follow   ⋮
@AGHuff

Fauci sits down, and people in the audience are saying:

"Nuremberg 2.0"

"You killed my grandmother"

A censored Doctor during the pandemic confronts Fauci after being proven right about the vaccinations, the masks, and social distancing. Those who refused to follow the governments orders have been vindicated completely in light of all the information that has come out. Those who think for themselves have won this battle.

"Everything I was censored on, I was proven to be right.

You said in an interview that an institution should make it hard for people to live their lives so they'd feel pressured to get vaccinated.

Plays audio where Fauci says that all objections to the Covid vaccinations were ideological bullshit

Are all objections to Covid vaccinations ideological bullshit doctor Fauci?

In reference to making it hard for people to get an education, traveling, and working I'd say it very much was in context. I take great offense to this.

I think America should take great offense to this.

Making it hard for people to live without getting a vaccination. You affected people's ability to work to flourish in American society. Shame on you.

Doctor Fauci, you've become doctor fear. Americans do not hate science. The American people hate having their freedoms taken from them. You inspired and created fear through mask mandates, school closures, and vaccine mandates that have destroyed the American people's trust in our public health institutions. This fear, you created, will continue to have ripple effects for generations to come. Quite frankly, you said, if you disagree with me you disagree with science. Doctor Fauci I disagree with you because I disagree with fear."

Overall, the public's reaction to the hearing reflects the deep polarization and ongoing debates surrounding the COVID-19 pandemic and its management. As discussions continue, it remains to be seen how these differing perspectives will shape public discourse and policymaking moving forward.

Conclusion

What's Next for Fauci?

As the hearings and discussions continue, Dr. Fauci's legacy remains a contentious topic. The hearings have shown us the deep political divisions over the pandemic response and highlighted the challenges faced by public health officials and the public in navigating this unprecedented crisis. Whether Fauci's explanations will put the controversies to rest or fuel further debates remains to be seen.

The testimony of Dr. Fauci before the House Select Subcommittee has reignited many debates about the COVID-19 pandemic and its management. While opinions are divided, it is clear that Dr. Fauci remains a pivotal figure in ongoing discussions.

This book aimed to provide a simple and clear explanation of recent events and the key issues involved. Whether you agree or disagree with Dr. Fauci, understanding the facts can help us all navigate these complex topics better.

Thank you for reading, and we hope this book has helped clarify why Dr. Fauci is once again in the headlines.